Innovative Parenting

Simple Tips for Raising Awesome Kids

JUDI HOLDEMAN

Illustrated by Rebecca Dame aged 13 and Hannah Dame aged 12

Printed in the United States of America.

ISBN   Paperback   978-1-64361-026-9
              Hardback   978-1-64361-027-6
              eBook   978-1-64361-028-3

Westwood Books Publishing LLC
10389 Almayo Ave, Suite 103
Los Angeles, CA 90064

www.westwoodbookspublishing.com

Peace on earth will come when all children
are raised with love and respect.

Contents

Introduction

Why did I choose this title for my book? In order to be the parents we want to be, we must be creative in ways that lead our children into a life of self-confidence and happiness, no matter how we might have been raised. When they are acting out is the moment in which we can choose to be inventive in our parenting. This is the time to pause for a moment and consider what effect our actions will have on our child and our relationship with them. It is important to act instead of react to their behavior. The tips in *Innovative Parenting* are for those times when you are wondering, "How can I lovingly guide my child?" This book has been written as a reference book, until the time a parent has learned to be on automatic regarding their positive parenting skills.

By the age of twenty-three, I had three children, a husband who did not know how to show his love to any of us, and I knew nothing about how to be a nurturing parent. I was raised in a dysfunctional home, was too young emotionally to be a mother, thought mostly of myself and my sorrows, and could not think of anything for which I was grateful, although I did have three beautiful babies.

When I was forty, I had the opportunity to become a mother for the fourth time. I made a commitment to myself and my unborn child that I would be a good parent. Over the years, I had observed all kinds of parenting, including my own, and know that using the tips in this little book can produce a child who becomes a responsible, loving adult. Parents are the child's first teachers; the child is the reflection of the parents. What a child learns in their formative years – mainly the first six years - lays the foundation for all that is to come.

The deep desires of our hearts are always supported and, lo and behold, a parenting class was being offered in the small town in which I lived. I enrolled as soon as I heard about it. What I learned in this class was very different from the kind of parenting I had received from my parents and had provided for my first three children. I had to put aside all I thought I knew and start from scratch in order to learn the rules of good parenting. This was easier than it might sound. Whenever my kid was doing something that was not acceptable, instead of immediately yelling at him, I would take a little pause and remind myself that I could not loose my temper and yell at my kid if I wanted him to live up to his full potential as a human being. I wholeheartedly desired to raise a child who would be a blessing to the world.

When he served two years as a Peace Corps Volunteer in a small country in Africa, I knew that I had attained my goal. His life partner tells me that my son has less parenting issues than anyone she has ever known. Over the years, I have watched my son grow into a caring and compassionate person. He is respectful of others, keeps his word, and is at peace with himself. When I was introduced to his employer, I was told that I had done a very good job raising him. The positive feedback I have received over the years about my son is what inspired me to write these tips for other parents.

The tips in this book are the ones I used. They became easy to follow out of my commitment to raising a happy, well-adjusted, 'tolerable' child. Many people I knew did not agree with the way I was raising my son. I had been told by the instructor of the parenting class that this might be the case. As my child was growing up, there were others who told me that he was the best kid they had ever been around; that he could play with their kid anytime. This assisted me in knowing that I was on the right track and kept me in alignment with the tips in this book. My first three children, whom I love dearly, did not have the advantages of positive parenting. This lack shows up in their lives today. It is my great sorrow that I cannot raise them again – I can only pass on what I have learned.

Love and Respect
(Cause and Effect)

The most important thing to remember when raising a child is that parenting follows the law of cause and effect. Parents are the cause and children express the effects. Any other way of looking at parenting is avoiding responsibility for being a parent. How a child turns out is primarily up to the parent(s), and being a single parent is no excuse for raising a rotten kid; many single parents raise great kids.

I do realize that some children are tougher to raise than others and a few tips along the way can act as a compass for any parent who realizes they may need assistance in being the great parent they want to be.

I certainly had to admit that I knew next to nothing about how to raise a happy, well-adjusted person. My own parents, who did give me some wonderful gifts, did not know how to nurture, and nurturing is a learned behavior. In fact, I did not even know the meaning of "nurturing." If you don't, you might want to look it up in a dictionary. My favorite definition is: raising someone to be an accepted member of the community. Over the years, I have taken it upon myself to learn how to be a nurturing person.

One lesson came from my only daughter. When she was grown, she told me that when she was little and got hurt, I never did "kiss it to make it well." I realized that I  never had. I just expected my first kids not to cry when they got hurt. I expected them to suck it up and shut up. That was how I was raised and I had no idea there was another way that would be nurturing to a child. I have learned that if I want to raise a child who is capable of being loving and nurturing, I must love and nurture that child. By treating our children with love and respect, we assist them in growing up to be loving people.

I still feel a twinge of anxiety when I make a request of someone and am belittled for wanting what I want. It's as if there is something wrong with me for wanting something they consider meaningless. I know this reflects how I was raised. I was raised to be obedient in a time when children's feelings were neither understood nor considered. We want our children to have respect; however, a child will not know what respect is if they do not receive it.

Respect is having courteous regard for the feelings or rights of others. This does not mean that we have to agree; just have regard for them. When a child is made to feel "less than" by something we say to them, this shows little respect for the child or their feelings about themselves. When I was a child, I recall being asked, "Who do you think you are?" in a very sarcastic tone by my mother when I wanted something with which she was not in agreement.

This would just tear me up inside and made me feel like I did not count.

While raising my son, I treated him as I would any other person with regard to his requests. After all, he was a person - just a little one – and someone I loved and cherished. This did not mean that he got what he wanted; it meant that he had a right to feel the way he did without being put down for his feelings or desires. Out of my respect for him, he grew up to be a respectful person.

Teasing a child is also being disrespectful of them and can be very hurtful to them. Teasing can make a child be mean to others and takes away their own self-respect. Making fun of a child's body parts – big ears, large feet, whatever – is not being kind to them. When we focus on what is beautiful about our child and complement that, we are increasing their self-esteem. I recall a story from when I was a child about a beautiful girl and an ugly princess. Everyone told the beautiful girl unkind things about herself and she grew up to be a not very nice person; the ugly princess was told how beautiful she was and she grew up believing in her own beauty and was kind to everyone. Little did I realize, when I was little, that this was a true story – a true story in how to treat children so that they do grow up to be beautiful and kind people.

It is my belief that raising a loving and respectful person is the greatest responsibility a parent has. When we do this, our children will be able to master their own lives on their own terms without bringing sorrow to anyone on the planet.

Baby is Crying

The following information, coming when I was expecting a baby, turned out to be the perfect tip to use for when and when not to let my baby cry. We condition our kids to cry or not just by knowing when to pick them up if they are crying. Here is what I learned and, boy, did it work!

Either pick up a crying baby immediately or do not pick them up at all. When we let a baby cry for awhile and then pick them up, this conditions them to cry until we do pick them up. Of course, when they have been sleeping and then wake up, they usually let us know they are awake by crying. Pick them up immediately. They may continue to cry because they are hungry or need to be changed; however, you are there with them and they don't connect that you are there because they cried.

When it is time for them to take a nap or go to bed at night and you have put them into their crib to sleep, they may cry. As long as you know that nothing is wrong, leave the room and let them cry themselves to sleep if that is what they need to do. Picking them up will simply teach them that crying results in being picked up. It won't be long before they quit crying when put to bed, since they have found out that it doesn't work.

When you know your child is sick and they awake in the night crying, pick them up immediately. If they are not sick and you know that nothing is wrong with them, you can make a choice to let them cry until they go back to sleep. My experience was that the longest my son cried when nothing was wrong with him was about one hour. He did this only a couple of times. He learned that, if nothing was wrong, I was not going to pick him up just because he was crying. This was a child who went to bed without any trouble from the time he was a very little guy. Bedtime was never a challenge.

He began sleeping the night through when he was about two months old because one night I was so tired that I completely missed his 2:00 a.m. feeding. He woke up and cried for about an hour and went back to sleep. His dad told me he did not wake me because he thought I heard him and was just letting him cry. He never again woke up for his 2:00 a.m. feeding.

A Positive Environment

This part is so easy; to raise your child in a positive environment. A positive environment is ten positives to four negatives. Just do the math. Sometimes my son would do something that pushed my buttons or I had to deal with him about something and did not do it in a positive way, or the negative way might be the only way to handle an issue. I would make up for the negatives by adding a few extra positives.

Stay conscious of the need for balance with a running mental chart estimating the number of positives vs. negatives during each day. When you become aware of having said so many negatives that the 10:4 ratio has become unbalanced, make a point of praising your child for something positive you noticed and did not comment about earlier, give a few extra hugs, tell them how proud you are of them, anything that will strike a positive note. If you keep this balance, your child's environment will be a positive one. And don't worry about having to be negative sometimes because sometimes it is necessary. You can always chunk in a few extra positives to make up for it.

Well, that's about it for raising a kid in a positive environment. Remember 10:4.

Positive Attention

When I was little myself, I recall hearing, "Oh, don't look at (or listen to) her; she just wants attention," like wanting attention was a bad thing. I grew up feeling guilty about wanting attention and wanting it anyway. Well, getting attention is the birthright of a child!!! That is why we had them, isn't it? To be with them and nurture their little lives until they can do it on their own?

A new baby gets a lot of the attention it needs while having diapers changed, being fed and held. As they grow a little, they require more attention in the first few years and until they become secure in the knowledge that you are there for them. A child who does not get the attention it requires will be the child who constantly demands attention because they are not getting the attention they need. There is a way to be sure your child gets enough attention and grows gently away from you until such time as they feel confident on their own.

Actually, listening to your child with that "inner" feeling will let you know when they need attention. They come around, want to be with you and have the expectation that you will be there for them whenever they want and need it. If they get pushed away too often because you are too busy or they get ignored a lot, you will notice that they will begin to do negative things such as crying, pulling on your clothes, throwing things around, bullying others and performing other negative forms of behavior attributed to a child. These behaviors are merely their means of saying, "I need your attention." As you may have heard before, "Negative attention is better than no attention at all." When they are receiving enough attention, a child will not do the negative things that they learn to do that solves their problem of getting enough attention.

When a child does not get enough attention, they let you know by demanding it. When a child is given all the attention it needs, they will not resort to negative behaviors for it. Pay a lot of attention to your child; as much as you can. If they squirm or try to get away, this is a good sign that their "attention tank" is full. Let them go. As they grow older, you will notice that they need less and less attention and will, in fact, begin to become less and less needful until you begin to wonder why they don't need you so much any more. When a child does this, you will know that you have given them the attention and security that they need to grow away from you. That is the whole purpose, right? To raise a child who is not dependent upon you; one who can go into the world and build a happy and successful life on their own.

The most important part of this "attention" thing is to pay attention to your child; when they want and need your attention and when they don't. This is part of being an "innovative" parent. Listen to them. Your child will let you know what they need by their behavior. In the long run, you both will be the one to benefit from the unspoken interchange of communication which underlies the actions of paying enough and not too much attention. You will have to give less and less attention as they grow from babies to young children; they will be on the road to facing the world from a secure place of belonging.

Kid Speak

This is one topic that is so important and yet there are just three things to say about the effects of how we applaud our children.

When your kid has done something for which you want to praise them, instead of saying "good boy" or "good girl," use the phrase "good job." The reasoning behind this is that telling them they are "good" implies that they can also be "bad." Out of this kind of speaking, they also learn not to take things personally. Don't we all wish we knew how not to take things personally? That we were raised knowing that people do not treat us they way they do because of who we are; that they treat us the way they do because of who they are?

The third effect is that kids, when being told they are doing a good job, get the idea that they are capable of doing well and this adds to their self-confidence and self-esteem. If they are not doing a good job, just show them how to do a good job. Remember, you are their first teacher. First say something like, "Here, let me show you what to do." Then say, "Good job."

Interrupting

Somehow we have been taught that interrupting someone is about as terrible as committing murder. How many times has someone yelled at you, "DON'T INTERRUPT!" We have been taught that it is rude, unconscionable and that we are being as bad as we can possibly be. Well . . . this is definitely a holdover from our own childhood. The problem is that, when a little child comes running up to us when we are busy talking to someone else, they want only a moment of our time and then they go right away again.

Personally, I think it shows disrespect to a child to make them wait five or ten minutes until we finish a conversation with someone else. How simple it is to just break away from our conversation, find out what they want (which takes about 15 seconds or less) and let them run back to whatever it was they were doing. As they grow older, it is appropriate to let them know not to interrupt when they can easily wait, if they want to begin a conversation of their own; however, a little kid just wants to say something quickly and get back to their own business.

I would suggest that you let your little kid interrupt when they just have a quick question and see how easy it is to answer them and get back to your own adult conversation. You will be surprised how easily life flows when your little child is not squirming around waiting for a chance to speak while you are in a long conversation. Try it. You'll like it.

Never Say "No"

Sounds crazy, huh? Read on.

Children only hear the command. **They do not hear** the words "no" or "don't." If a child is expected to do what they are told, they need to be given a command that they can understand. They do want to please us. Children need to be told what we want them to do – **not** what we don't want them to do. Directing children in this positive manner enables them to follow our direction.

Examples:

1. My child is opening a drawer and I don't want him in it. If I say, "Don't open the drawer," all he hears is "Open the drawer." If I say, "Please close the drawer," he hears "Close the drawer."
2. My child is running by the side of the pool. If I say, "Don't run," all she hears is "Run." If I say, "Please walk," she hears "Walk."

Often the command needs to be repeated more than once because children want to think that they have a choice in the matter. Once they have heard the command, they *will* follow it and sometimes not immediately. Not obeying immediately is their way of making minding their own choice and feeling like they have some control over their own lives. And if their choice is your choice, isn't that a good thing? Even if it takes a few seconds or so?

Example:

My child is throwing food from the highchair to the floor. If I say, "Please keep your food on the tray," she might throw some onto the floor once more. When this happens, I notice that right before she did this, she hesitated for a moment to see what I would do. If she gets a reaction from me, she will do it again and again and the battle is on. If I stay cool and firmly repeat the command of "Please keep your food on the tray," she will hesitate again and then follow the instruction. That hesitation is the moment of choice for a child.

Another fascinating aspect of the word "no" occurs when a three-year-old begins to say it. This child is not saying "no" with our meaning. They are saying, "I'm not you," as they begin to assert their own individuality. When this happens, just say "okay." Scary, huh? . . . saying "okay" to a three-year-old who is saying "no." In this context, "okay" means "I hear you;" it does not mean you agree. By this age, a child has begun to realize that if they say "no," they are creating all kinds of excitement – parents getting upset and giving them all kinds of (negative) attention. A simple "okay" will diffuse a child's "no." They will get that you know they are not you and that you expect them to follow your instruction, perhaps with assistance.

An aspect of a three-year-old that also needs understanding is that, when they appear to refuse to do what they are asked, it is a good idea to go to them and gently guide them in what you want them to do. With this guidance, they learn that you mean business and that they will not get away with not minding.

Examples:

1. The child has been asked to get dressed. She says "no." Say "okay" and lead her to her clothes, ignoring the "no." Ask if she needs assistance. Allow her to make the choice of putting on her clothes. If she balks and it appears that she is not going to mind, gently give the assistance she needs to complete the task of getting dressed, repeating the command: "It's time to get dressed now." Once she sees who is in charge and that it  is not her, she will get dressed, with or without assistance. Remember, a parent who is upset by a child's negative behavior is a parent who has handed control over to their kid.

2. You ask your small son to "come here." He says "no." Say "okay" and then go towards him, take his hand and lead him gently to where you want him to go. Be firm and kind at the same time.

Hint: When I first began saying what I wanted my son to do instead of what I didn't want him to do, I had to stop and think about the positive way in which to say what I wanted; to say it without using the words "no" or "don't." This did not come naturally to me; yelling did. This is when I had to think of the phrase, "It's not what we say but how we say it." It's okay to take a moment in your head to phrase what you want to say so that it comes out as a positive direction, with love in your voice, and still stand firm. This is the innovative part – to take the time to use your imagination to come up with the positive way of saying what you want to say to your kid. After a bit of practice, I found it became easier all the time to come up with positive commands.

EXCEPTION TO THE "NEVER SAY NO" RULE: There is a time that it is okay to say "no" and is strongly recommended. When a child wants something and you do not want them to have it or do it, just say "no." No explanations; just "no." In this context, "no" is the only appropriate answer. If you give a reason, they can then begin an argument with you about whatever it is they want. Once you have said "no," stick to it. If you change your mind, you are in big trouble. They learn that, if they just ask enough, you will say "yes." Oops, that is one of the biggest mistakes you can make. So, "no" means "no." Once they know that you mean it when you say it, once is all you will have to say it – and many arguments will never even begin.

Ignore Negative Behavior

No matter how much positive attention a child receives, they do have a tendency to do things that are not considered acceptable behavior. I think that is one reason they have parents; to teach them how to be successful living in the world. Negative behaviors do not get us too far in getting along with others as we go along in life.

Every child goes through a stage of throwing a fit to get what they want. If throwing that fit does not work, they have a tendency not to throw another one, at least at home where the first fit is usually performed. When my youngest threw his first fit, I just ignored him and walked away. Pretty soon, when he saw that he got no attention, he just shut up and went on with his day. I don't recall that he ever threw another one at home. However, when the fit at home with no audience except a parent or two doesn't get any results, they seem to like to try again by going to the next level and throw one in public to see if they can get different results.

I recall each of my children had one episode (and only one, I might add), when we were shopping and they decided they wanted me to buy them something to which I told them "no." Wow! Did that cause a total upset for them! They screamed, cried, threw a fit and kept insisting I buy them what they wanted. I totally ignored them. I recall that one of them just lay down on the floor of the store while pitching their little fit. I finished paying for the groceries I was buying and began walking out of the store. They got up, shut up and followed me out the door. I even got the feeling that they may have been a little embarrassed at their own behavior, as little as they were. Anyway, they never did that again.

Once a child realizes that, if they just throw a fit, they will get what they want, believe me, they will continue that behavior forever. Ignoring their fits takes all the fun out of their throwing them.

Other negative behavior can be something as simple as (an example) scratching between their legs which, as we all know, is not considered appropriate public behavior. My son had the chicken pox and would scratch between his legs because it itched there. I was the one who had the fit and continued to harp at him not to scratch there. Little did I know that he would continue this behavior into adulthood and, so far as I know, still does it, although not in a very noticeable way. I notice it particularly because I recall how much I nagged him about it and kept checking to see if he was still doing it. I know that my attention on this behavior is what kept him doing it long after he quit itching.

Touching Everything!

Has the time yet come when your little kid begins to want to touch everything? If not, get ready, because just about the time they learn to pull themselves up onto a piece of furniture, you will see them begin to reach for whatever object is within touching distance. Children are the original "Curious George." What looks like they want to attack everything is really that they want to know what it is, how it feels, sometimes even what it tastes like. When a child gets to touch, hold and know everything within their reach, they usually don't bother those objects again. Their curiosity has been satisfied.

Slapping a young kid's hand and yelling "no" at them whenever they reach for something is upsetting to both the child and the adult; it certainly is not a very loving thing to do. It also does not really do any good because, if you will notice, they just try again. They still want to examine the object. When my son was at this stage, I let him touch, hold and get to know everything while I sat with him through this processing of "things." Once he got to know an object, he rarely, if ever, touched it again. I did remove anything from his reach that I did not want damaged and, when he was past the "touch everything" stage, put those things back where I wanted them. I think this was when he was about three years old. By then he was into playing with his own toys and left mine alone.

Another interest that a young child will develop is "what is in that drawer or behind that door," especially in the kitchen. You won't even be able to fix a meal without your kid opening the cabinet doors and dragging out whatever they can. This is the time to plan a "kitchen exploration." Take everything out of every bottom cabinet and drawer (one at a time) that is within their reach. Let them examine the contents of that cabinet or drawer and then replace the items. They just want to know what is in there and this will satisfy their curiosity. Then prepare one lower cabinet that your child can call their own. Put in plastic and any other unbreakable items that it's okay for them to touch. Let them know that this is their special space. Next time you are in the kitchen to cook or whatever and they head for the cabinets, direct them to their cabinet. If they head for yours, let them know that those are your "special" and they have their own. You will be surprised at how they will "get it."

The "Wonderful" Twos

I call this third year of a child's life the wonder year - the age between two and three. If you will take notice sometime around their second birthday, you will see your child seem to – all of a sudden – open their eyes and say to themselves (I am sure of this), "Oh look, there is a world out there. Let me have at it!" And then the fun begins. This year of a child's life is the most formative of all the years. This is the year that, using the information given in this chapter, will make all the difference in whether or not your kid is a rebellious teenager. Believe it or not.

When my son was 11 years old, he went to live with his dad. This was his choice. I was curious as to how his teenage years would be without me, since I had raised him in his "wonder" year in the way I will share with you, and wanted to be with him during his last years at home. As it turned out, because of how I had treated him when he was two, he did just fine without me.

Teenage rebellion begins with an adolescent wanting to control their own life and, if they did not get to before, they are definitely going to do so now. Many of the tips in this book are intended to guide parents in letting their children have age-appropriate degrees of control throughout their childhood. By gradually letting go, you can raise kids who won't have to rebel. If a child has nothing to rebel against, they won't do rebellion. By the time they reach their teens, they will be making most of their own choices. They may even come to you for brainstorming a difficult issue because of the trust you have built with them over their growing-up years.

When your two-year-old begins their great and wonderful adventure of checking out the world, they have reached the stage where they realize there is more to life than mommy and daddy. It's like they wake up and want to go for it - whatever "It" is. And "It" is just about everything. They want to investigate, check out their own power, and experience their own lives. Of course, they need to be guided and, at the same time, not held back from their experiences. The way to do this is to let them do what they want to do and be there for them; catch them if they fall. Unless of course, what they want to do would be dangerous to their physical well-being; kept from doing non-dangerous things is dangerous to their mental health. Doing as much as they can safely do builds self-esteem in a kid. They get to experience, at a young age, their wonderful capabilities while, at the same time, get to have some control over themselves.

When my son was two years old, we were at a friend's house. He decided to climb along a ladder that had been placed vertically over their driveway which reached from the sidewalk to the top of the garage which was under the first story of their house. The ladder was easily accessible at ground level and lay on a ledge at the top of the garage which was about eight feet above ground level. My son decided to walk across this ladder. My first inclination was to run after him, yelling at him to stop before he got hurt, etc. Taking a deep breath, I walked onto the slanting

driveway and paced myself to go along with him walking the ladder above me. Were he to fall, I knew I could catch him. He walked without falling and I had him jump into my arms, when he reached the end of the ladder that lay eight feet off the ground. We both felt great! He was grinning and I was glad he made it.

Another time, I was using a small but sharp knife to cut some cardboard and he wanted to "help mommy." I used my parenting philosophy on this one; let him do what he can do. I was right there so I gave him the knife, gave him explicit instructions and watched him carefully to see that he was using it properly. He was almost three years old, at the time. He was doing a great job when the phone rang. I left him to his cutting for just a moment to grab the phone. He took this moment to accidentally make a small cut on his finger which bled profusely. From this experience, he learned to respect knives and I learned that it's okay for a child to get hurt a little bit in order to learn a big lesson.

As a parent, it is our job to assess a situation and, if little or no harm can be done to themselves or anyone else, let the kid do it. You will be so blessed to have a kid that is not afraid to live and, at the same time, loves the experience of learning who they are and what they can do. And this teenager will be a happy, well-adjusted person who just goes out and lives without causing damage to themselves or others. What more could you want?

Giving Kids Choices

There comes the time in the life of a young child when they no longer accept what you give them and want something different. This might begin by something as simple as balking at eating what you give them for breakfast. When this happens, you know that they are ready to begin making some choices about their own lives. This is a very healthy thing for a child to do. Making choices is the way a human being begins to take control of their own lives. A child who is not allowed to make choices of their own about their own life is the adult who spends their life trying to get it by controlling others.

So here is how it works. You give your kid oatmeal for breakfast and they say they do not want oatmeal. This is a new behavior on their part because they have never expressed that they wanted anything different from what you have served them for breakfast; this is your clue that they are ready to begin making choices. Say okay and ask them if they would like raisin bran or oatmeal (or any two things you know they like). This next part is very important: Give them only a choice between two items that you don't care which one they choose. They get to choose and you get to guide their choices.

As time goes by, your child will begin to want to make their own choices about a lot of things. Just remember to give them a choice between two things that you like or of two things that you don't care which one they pick. In this way, they learn to make good choices for themselves because you are there to guide them and, at the same time, they feel that they have some control over their own life.

I once knew a woman who asked her two-year-old what she wanted for breakfast every morning. She thought that she was doing the right thing by letting her kid choose. Believe me, her kid didn't care. I was there once and watched this procedure. The kid looked so stressed about having to make a decision about what to have for breakfast and, I could tell, would rather have just had her breakfast put in front of her without having to make this broad decision for herself at her age. By the age of seven, this little girl had childhood diabetes. I have often wondered if this was caused by the stress of having to make so many choices in her young life before she was ready and with no guidance from her parent.

Another mother I knew who was into "giving her kid choices," took her young child shopping for shoes and told her to pick the ones she wanted out of the whole range of shoes in the store. The mother wanted the kid to have some practical new shoes. The child picked red ones covered with shinny red sequins. (As a little kid, I would have picked them, too.) Had the mother picked out two pair of shoes that she liked and then told the child to pick one, the child would have felt that they made the choice and the mother would have gotten the practical shoes that she wanted for her kid.

Listen to your child. They will let you know when they are ready to made choices. They begin with little ones and grow into the bigger ones all on their own. They do not need to be pushed into making choices; they need to be allowed to make them with your guidance of "this or that" so they learn to make wise choices. The child who is guided in making wise choices continues to make wise choices into adulthood.

Discipline

Spanking our kids, beating them, hitting them, yelling at them does not show them that we love them. But, you say, "What about spare the rod and spoil the child?" Well, in the 'olden days' when that idea was put forth, the rod was used as an analogy to guidance. The shepherd's rod, to which this refers, was long and ended with a circular hook. This hook was used by putting it around the neck of a sheep and gently guiding it away from a cliff when it got too close to the edge. A way to rephrase this piece of advice is "children need guidance."

Actually, discipline is a form of guidance and there are gentle ways to guide that teach consequences for actions. One way, and the best way of which I know, is to send your child to its room for their unacceptable behavior. When the issue of sending a child to its room comes up, I have noticed time and again people not wanting to do this. Some of their arguments are that the kid will just play with their toys, watch TV, etc. Because being sent to their room begins the first time a child needs firm discipline, they are so young that they do not think about playing. Because of what you will say to them when they are sent to their room, they will be thinking about what they did. Just go ahead and follow this discipline procedure. Believe me; you will be glad you did.

I would not presume what rules to make regarding your child's behavior; I can tell you how to enforce the rules you do make. Kids need to have boundaries and, at the same time, a large enough playing field so that they can be who they are within these boundaries. A kid with no boundaries is one who will rule the roost. A kid with too small a field in which to play will turn rebellious.

When your kid is doing something that is not acceptable, tell them that what they are doing is "unacceptable behavior" and not to do it again. Everyone should get one chance. Know that they will do it again. Children love to test us to be sure that we keep our word; that we mean what we say. When they do it again, here is an outline of a procedure you can follow:

1. "Johnny/Susie, I have told you not to _____. That is unacceptable behavior. Now go to your room for two minutes. Think about what I have told you. When the timer rings, you can come out." (Be specific so they know what it is they have done that they are not supposed to do and BE BRIEF. After the first five words or so, kids tune out and don't hear you anymore, anyway.)

2. Take them to their room, if they do not go on their own, and shut the door. Once they

know you mean business, they will go on their own. Set the timer for two minutes and place it where they can hear it when it rings.

3. When they come out, never refer to the incident again. Unless, of course, they do it again. Then it's a whole new ball game. They may test that behavior again; however, as a rule, they only get sent to their room once or twice for the same thing. If they do it again, start over with item 1 above.

Sometimes, when a child is acting out, it is easy to get upset with them. Sending them to their room also gives us a "time out" away from them so that we can calm down. In the beginning, two minutes is quite a long time for little kids. As they get older, you can decide on the seriousness of the rules' violation. I recommend two minutes for minor, five minutes for medium and ten minutes for major infractions of the rules.

Sometimes I had to send my son to his room for different unacceptable behaviors more than once a day. It's okay to send them whenever they need it. I think the most times I ever had to enforce the rules this way was four in one day. That was many more than were usual. There were many days he never got sent to his room at all. Also, I never threatened him that I would send him to his room, if he didn't quit whatever it was he was doing; I always sent him there for unacceptable behavior and/or disobeying my rules. Kids are very smart. They know what they are not supposed to do.

There is another form of discipline that I used successfully when my son would do something totally outrageous that he absolutely knew he should not do. He would test me to see if he could get away with some kind of rebellious behavior. For this I would take away a privilege that he valued in order to keep him appraised of the fact that I would not put up that particular behavior. I seldom had to do this. One time he missed a birthday party because of something he had done. Another time, I sent him to bed with no dinner. That was pretty drastic; however, what he had done was way out of line. After sending him to bed for the evening, I began to feel really bad. Then I had to realize that, if I changed my mind, he would learn that he could not count on me to keep my word and would try to get away with other such behavior. Consistency is very important.

What I learned from that experience was to only give him a consequence that I would not later regret. In the heat of the moment, this is not always easy to do. I began stopping and taking a few deep breaths before meting out a consequence. Another "innovative parenting" hint: Take a short time to think of a consequence that would not be detrimental to either you or your child.

Protecting Your Child

It is really okay to protect your kids from things that are harmful to them. This means other kids, adults, poor food choices, unsafe toys, violent television shows and anything else that comes along that would damage them, either mentally or physically. A parent is the best advocate a child has. Never be afraid to stand up for your kid. Do it firmly, gently and with grace in a loving manner. This is one way kids can learn what is good for them and what isn't, without being exposed to anger in order to do what is right. Since parents are a kid's first teacher, it is from the parent that the kid learns to stand up and defend him/herself without hating others.

Meanwhile, we don't want to make our kids afraid of other people while protecting them. I have seen people make their kids afraid of other people by telling them not to speak to strangers. One day while out shopping, I saw the cutest little fellow and said "hello" to him. He got a frightened look on his face and ran to his mother, hiding his face in her skirt. This kid was terrified. I don't believe this is a way to protect our kids.

Something we can do is suggest to our kid that they do not go anywhere with someone they don't know. This can be told to them when they are old enough to be on their own while going to school or other places. Meanwhile, keep your little kids close to you when out in public and make sure you know where they are. I recall reading a sign in a restaurant that said, "Strangers are friends we haven't met yet." I think this is a good motto by which to raise our kids and, at the same time, watch out for them when we take them places.

Keeping Your Kid Honest

Children are not born liars. So why does a person lie? Have you ever given that much thought? I have, and the conclusion I have made is that I lie in order not to get in trouble. I'll bet that is why you might lie, too. Think about it. By the time I was a young adult, lying was just a habit for me and was one of the things I had to put away as childish behavior. So . . . why did I become a liar?

When I was little, did something I was not supposed to do and my dad found out about it, I would get in so much trouble that I learned not to tell the truth. Liars are made; not born. With this realization, I set out to create a child who was not afraid to tell the truth.

I did it, Mom!

One time I left a glass jar on the porch. My son was about four years old. He messed with the jar and I found pieces of it all over the grass. I knew that he was the one who had broken it. Up to this point, I had always praised him for telling the truth and not disciplined him in any way for doing something he was not supposed to do, when he was truthful about it. I would let him know that he wasn't supposed to do what he did but he did not get in trouble for doing it; I would praise him for telling me the truth about whatever he had done. Well, I asked him about the broken jar. Had I broken a jar, when I was little, I would probably have undergone bodily harm. Without any hesitation, he said, "I broke it, Mom." I was so proud of him for telling me the truth. I was so proud of me for never giving him a bad time for whatever he had done when he told me the truth, even though there were times when I was pretty upset about something he had done.

Always telling the truth to our children is also important. The facilitator of the parenting class included that we should not lie to them about Santa Claus, the Easter Bunny, the Tooth Fairy and such others. This did not sit well with me, at first; however, I wanted so much to do the right thing with my son that I did follow this advice and was not sorry. I told my son that Santa Claus was the spirit of Christmas. The funny thing was that he had heard about Santa Claus from others, wanted to believe he was real and chose to do so, in spite of me. I did not contradict him and he did not carry that big disappointment of finding out Santa Claus really was just a story, when the time came that he realized it was. He also knew that I would never lie to him about anything.

Another thing that most kids do is steal something from a store. They do this sometime about the age of five. One day we were at a grocery store. You know those jars of stuff and candy bars on shelves about kid level that entice them to ask you to buy something? Well, he took a handful of jelly beans out of one of the jars, brought it over to me with a sly look in his eye and said, "Look what I have, Mom." I told him that he was not supposed to take things that did not belong to him; that this was stealing. I took him over to the store manager and told him to tell the manager what he hand done. I stood back and watched. The manager thanked him for giving them back. My son walked back over to me.

I went over to the store manager and told him to really lay it on him; that he had been too nice about it. He took my son up to his office and came down with him a little bit later. My son looked scared to death. When we left the store, I asked him what had happened. He told me "the man" took his picture and was angry with him for taking the jellybeans; that he was really in a lot of trouble. That was the first and last time my son stole anything. He was also so embarrassed/ashamed/scared (I was never sure which) that he would never go into that store again.

The conclusions to be drawn from this chapter are:

- Never get mad at your kid for telling the truth. Praise them for it. Support them in how you want them to be, without anger.
- When they (in their fifth year or whenever) first steal something from a store or someone, turn them in and let the store manager or person handle it in such a way that it scares them a lot. P.S. If they are already at home when you discover the "stolen goods," let the store manager know you are coming back and for them to take a hard line with your child. Take the kid back to the store with what

they stole (usually candy). Have them confess to the manager. If they refuse and within the child's hearing, tell the manager to call the police and start to walk away. Your kid will really feel the pressure and will confess. I guarantee it. (This is a true story of what another parent I know did.) Better to be scared caught stealing at five than be in jail at twenty-five. Believe me, this will be a great deterrent. And remember – stay mellow.

Time to Get Up

This little tip is one that made a really huge difference in my life with my son. When he began school and I would go in to wake him up, he would act like children all seem to do. He did not want to get up. How usual – ha, ha. Well, I put on my thinking cap and came up with the following plan. It totally worked!!!

I bought a digital alarm clock and put it by his bed. Mind you, he was in kindergarten by then and could read numbers. He felt like a big kid by having his own clock. I set it for the time he had to get up and showed him how it worked. Then I told him it was his job to get up when the alarm sounded, turn it off and get himself dressed. When he was dressed, his next job was to wake me up. He loved this and we never had to play the game  called "Time to Get Up," along with the ensuing battles over the years, which I have noticed other parents playing with their kids.

Sharing and Taking Turns

Often we are afraid of raising children who are selfish and don't want to share. . . so we **make** them share without giving them the chance to share on their own. This is really not necessary.

When I first heard about the idea of giving a kid the choice of sharing something they had, I had reservations; however, I felt I owed it to my kid to give him a chance. My first experience of allowing my son to share on his own was a real eye-opener. We were together with a friend and her little girl. My son had some cookies. My friend's little girl saw the cookies and wanted one. I asked my son if he wanted to share a cookie with her. I watched him pause. I could tell that he was thinking about it. After a few seconds, he handed her a cookie. I had heard that, given the chance, a child would share; when forced to do so, they didn't like it. This turned out to be so true. I never forced him to share and he always did, unless it was something very special to him.

I think there is some innate understanding in all humans about the meaning of "my special." It certainly does show up in children. There definitely is a time to share and a time not to share. A time not to share, for a kid, is their birthday presents before they have had a chance to play with them.

I recall a time when my son was having a birthday party and in the middle of opening his presents, another kid wanted to begin playing with one that had already been opened. I found myself saying, "No. That is his special." One of the mothers sort of looked at me like I should let this other kid play with the toy but the kid understood and did not press the issue. In fact, he even nodded and said okay in a very knowing way. Every kid understands that their new presents are "special."

There were other times, after that incident, when I would tell a kid that whatever it was they wanted was my son's "special" and they totally understood. I have even used that on adults about my own stuff and they easily understand that concept. I bet you do, too!

Taking turns is another way of sharing. Maybe there is only one of something. Your kid and their friend or sibling both want to play with it at the same time. I recall teaching taking turns, when my son was about two years old. I was taking care of a friend's child for a few hours. It was wintertime. I had made a darling macramé swing which I hung in the kitchen so my kid could swing and stay warm playing inside. Both kids, of course, wanted to swing and it was only big enough for one. As I had learned in the parenting class, I put one of them on the swing and set the timer for two minutes. The other was kind of upset because they wanted to swing. I just held the kid who wasn't swinging and explained to them that, when the timer rang, it would be their turn. When the timer sounded, I took the first kid off and put the other kid in the swing, set the timer for two minutes and comforted the kid who had to get off the swing. In the beginning, there was a little upset on the part of each kid; however, they soon realized that

they were each going to get another turn and settled in to enjoy the ride.

For a little kid, two minutes is a long time. Each got a time to swing and the other didn't have to wait too long for their turn. This worked perfectly. It also taught them about taking turns. There were other instances, when I was caring for other children, that I used this taking-turns technique with other toys. As long as it is fair (equal time and not too long), kids are okay with about anything. Happy is the child who knows how to take turns.

Quality Time

When parents are working, they don't really have a lot of time for their kids. Finding time to spend with them, time that they will love being with you, is so easy, whether you are working or not. In short, it is called: "Doing chores together." Not only will you be spending quality time with your kid, they will simultaneously be in training for adulthood.

Okay, I said this will be easy; however, there are ways to go about this that make it fun for everyone, too. In the first place, sharing chores with a parent is a lot different than a parent saying something like, "Go make your bed." When it's time to make beds, take your kid with you and make your bed together. Then go make their bed together. Gently train them in how to make a bed. At first, it will not be the perfect way to make a bed because they will be so little. Whatever the finished bed looks like, just leave it. They will be so proud that they have done this job and, if you later change it to make it look better, the message they will get is that they didn't do it good enough and loose interest in making beds. And they *will* notice if you change it. If you can't handle the way your bed looks when you are finished bed-making together, just make their bed with them. You will be surprised how soon they will make a bed as well as you do, once they are older.

Now you get to pick up their toys and neaten up their room together, cook together, wash dishes together, do laundry together, clean the bathroom together, dust and vacuum together, mown the lawn together, sweep the sidewalk together, etc. You get the idea. What joy for a kid to share in all of these chores because they are with you. They will feel needed and you will be delighted at what they can do. As they grow older, you will come to know for which jobs they are ready. Pretty soon, you will both be doing all the work around the house, you will be spending quality time with your kid and no one will become resentful about having to do it all. Just remember to be patient because it will take longer to do chores with them, at first. However, because this will be spending quality time with your kid, you won't have to take the time you don't have to do it later. This will enable both parent and kid to have alone time, too, knowing that you have spent so much time together.

Another way to spend quality time is watching TV together. This is a good idea so that, no matter what is on, you can be the discerning voice about what they are watching. Actually, this can be another way to give your input as to your values, beliefs and attitudes about life.

Because you are doing chores together, you will have time to watch TV together and do all the other fun things in life that kids really enjoy like playing games, riding bicycles, taking hikes, etc. Have fun with your kid. They really do grow up fast. And a happy kid is a good kid!!!

Perfect Parenting

Just for the record, I have to let you know that there is no such thing as perfect parenting. We can follow all the suggestions in this little book, memorize every chapter, take all the advice others have to give us, read other parenting books, etc., etc., etc., and still will not be a perfect parent . . . so relax. We will do things to and around our children for which we are sorry and ashamed and wonder at ourselves that we would do them, feel guilty for doing them and wonder what harm we have done to our little one. There is something I used to do with my kid, when I was a jerk parent, which I know kept his little spirit open and loving;

something that kept him from being afraid of me when I blew it and performed random acts of unkindness towards him.

When my behavior to him was unacceptable (in my opinion), I would go to him and tell him I was sorry for what I had done. I would be specific so that he would know exactly what I was talking about. One time, I was upset about something he did and bopped him on the head. He cried and ran to his room. I waited until I had myself under control, after beating myself up for doing what I did to him, and went into his room. He was on his bed. I sat down beside him and told him I was sorry that I had lost it and hit him on the head. I told him I should not have done that. I hugged him and asked him to forgive me. He did.

Over the years, I had to do this more than a few times for things I did not like that I had done to him. Yelling at him was another thing I had to ask him to forgive. He always forgave me. I believe my being human with him instead of having the attitude that I was the parent and he was the kid and that everything I did was right is one of the reasons he is such a great person today. When I first began doing this, it was not easy. My ego certainly did not like it. When I saw the positive difference it made in him when I told him I was wrong, it just became another way of being with him. It was worth it to admit to him that I was not perfect and he knew me as someone who really cared about him.

List of Parenting Tools Needed

1. A minute timer that makes a loud sound when the time is up.
2. That's all folks!!!

P.S. Adding a Kid

The following tip is not one I learned in the parenting class I took. I picked this one up in 1960 when I was pregnant with my second child in an article I read in the doctor's office waiting room. It worked wonders in assisting my first kid's possibly feeling that he had been replaced by the second kid and avoided that dreaded happening known as "sibling rivalry."

Before the birth of the second child, buy a rubber baby doll that can be fed, bathed and diapered. It needs to be clothed, wrapped in a blanket and equipped with a feeding bottle. Upon arrival home with the new baby, have someone else carry the new baby into the house and put it down, perhaps in its crib or another room. The older kid needs to see you without the new baby when you first get home. Since you have been away for some time, go straight to the older kid, hug them, hold them and tell them how much you have missed them. Then tell them that you have brought them a present. Give them the doll and let them know that this is their very own baby.

Now is the time to introduce the older child to the new one. Still sitting with them, have the person who brought in the new baby bring it over and let them hold it before they ever see you hold it. In this way, they can identify with the new baby before they have a chance to identify it with you. This form of introduction to the new sibling will take care of a lot of the feeling of being replaced the older child might possibly have.

After you have greeted your older kid and they have been introduced to the new baby, it is now safe to take care of the new one. Invite the older kid to participate. When it's time to feed the baby, have the older kid feed their baby; when it's time to bathe the new baby, they get to bathe their baby; when you dress the new baby, they dress their baby. I am sure you get the idea. As you will come to see, they will gradually be less and less interested in taking care of their baby and go on to playing with other toys, leaving you alone to care for the new baby.

Whenever possible, make sure the older kid gets recognized by others before they begin to make over the new baby. This will also assist in preventing those feelings of being replaced. You may want to let someone make over the new baby first just to watch the look on the face of the older child. It is very interesting to see their reaction; somehow it shows in their face that something is amiss. One way to handle it, when others make a fuss over the new baby before acknowledging the older kid, is to bring in the older kid by using inclusive words like "Tell Aunt Mary about our new baby" or "Uncle Jim wants to know what you did today." This will bring attention to the older child who needs to know that they still count.

CPSIA information can be obtained
at www.ICGtesting.com
Printed in the USA
LVHW041917211019
634862LV00002B/533/P